BROADW~ NG, INC.

TRANSIENTS WELCOME

Three One-Act Plays by

Rosalyn Drexler

249 WEST 29 STREET NEW YORK NY 10001 (212) 563-3820

First printing: August 1984

ISBN: 0-88145-019-7

Cover Art by Michael Bartalos
Design by Marie Donovan
Set in Baskerville by L&F Technical Composition, Lakeland, FL
Printed and bound by BookCrafters, Inc., Chelsea, MI

CONTENTS

PREFACE

Jack Kroll

After all the labels have dried up and blown away—Theatre of the Absurd, Black Comedy—what's left is vision and power. Such is the case with Rosalyn Drexler, Ionesco, Beckett, N.F. Simpson, playwrights who delight in pulling the lines of reality askew on a stage. Yet there is no one quite like Rosalyn Drexler. It's easy for some artists not to be themselves; for Drexler it's impossible. If she reminds us of other writers it's because she embodies the universe they write about. She is one of those artists who writes out of a kind of explosive helplessness before the sheer nature of life itself. The world does something and Drexler responds with a rippling, muscular reflex of words, working intuitively, and with immense respect for her craft. Some artists go looking for trouble; they bushwack reality, determined to make a score. Drexler minds her own business, which is her readiness to respond—this is the primal readiness of the artist, but there's nothing primitive about it. Drexler has the cursed self-awareness of the contemporary artist. These three one-act plays constitute a triple meditation on the polluting presence of the artist. The artist pollutes reality, but reality pollutes the artist; it's a reciprocal corruption that crystallizes the flawed diamonds of consciousness. Transients Welcome, says Drexler's signpost; artists are the transients, the seedy bag persons of reality who quiver in their rooms, sorting out the tainted glories of their shaping sensibilities. The bad conscience of art is old news now, the bad conscience of consciousness itself is upon us.

Every slob in the street has become a Henry James, tainted by the least speck of self-awareness. We are all too sensitive for our own good, whether we speak in conditional clauses or in a salvo of obscenities. The artist of this moment knows he's a clown; his strategy is the creation of a complex facetiousness

encoded by technology. These three poignant plays are
Drexler's savage and sorrowful elegy for the artist, the
psychic consumptive whose magic mountain has become a
radioactive landfill.

Art can't help being about art now; pastiche is at the
center because human beings have become pastiches in the
secular supermarket of world culture. When the confident
neoclassicist Landor brought together disparate figures in
his *Imaginary Conversations*, he created magisterial rap-
sessions between competing but reinforcing world-pictures.
In Drexler's plays, artists and their creations stumble upon
one another like drunks lurching into the wrong motel room.
In *Room 17C* she throws together Kafka and Arthur Miller
like some mad scientist mixing the dubious contents of two
testtubes. Here, Kafka's cockroach Gregor Samsa becomes
Sammy Gregor, meeting up with Willy Loman's wife, Linda,
who herself has gone out on the road. This kind of meeting is
Drexler's way of squeezing some additional use-value out of
an artist's creations, as well as probing the ambiguities of art
itself. So, Willy's long-suffering wife pulls out of her own
play and goes off on her own. And Kafka's self-loathing bug
is a reasonably satisfied professional; infestor of crummy
hotel rooms, "loathsome and lonesome." Their dialogue
becomes a meeting of minds, bodies, and carapaces. Sammy
is the most idealistic of cockroaches. "I am a Utopian
quester," he says passionately to Linda. "You are Utopia;
however, I know when to back off."

The question in all of these plays is whether art should
back off, if only as a strategic move to its pushing forward
with cleaned hands and charged batteries. Linda, attracted
by Sammy's ardor but repelled by his bugginess, treats him
like the masochist she know most lovers—and artists—to be.
"Ah, poetry, the deadly stranger in our midst," says Sammy after Linda has slugged him with her shoe. "You, a bug,
raise my spirits," admits the divided Linda, comparing him
with her beaten-down husband, "who does not love life."
Sammy is in fact a kind of artist, a floorbound troubadour
who can sing an ode to his own lowliness. As a former human,

he's an expert on the inhumanity of artists who, as he points out, get their blood from paint tubes and inkwells. Sammy indeed shows more humanity than Linda's (and Willy's) son Joey, who's appalled by Linda's dalliance with the verminous Sammy. "What does he have that Dad doesn't?" he demands. "Feelers," replies Linda; "Looks aren't everything." In the end it's Sammy who survives the apocalypse, singing a roachy transmutation of "America the Beautiful" and admitting, "Of course I lack imagination. Lucky for me. Imagination can accomplish the end of the world."

Yes, this is where the road of heightened consciousness, exemplified by the artist, inevitably leads. In *Lobby*, an aging Southern belle named Blanche admits that "The streetcar has been renamed: Despair." In her original incarnation in Tennessee William's play she was a sensitive creature savaged by brutes in a world bereft of art. In *Lobby* she hooks up with Oscar Wilde, supreme advocate of art for art's sake, and it doesn't improve her destiny appreciably. This play takes place in a joint like New York's Chelsea Hotel, a shrine begrimed with the miseries and splendors of generations of artists—the very opposite of the fashionable Cadogan Hotel in London, where Oscar was arrested and started on his journey to disgrace and death. In *Lobby* the exquisite and ironic Oscar shares a greasy burger with the fastidious Blanche, whom he tells, "I could have asked them to hold the mayo, madame, if I had known of your preference." Oscar's fight has always been to insulate himself from the chaotic flux of life, unlike Teddy, the junky whom Drexler introduces, whose girlfriend Estralita says, "Teddy likes things the way they are— shitty." Both Blanche and Oscar are helpless against this rising tide of putrescence, the decayed distillation of a transcendent energy whose defeat is also the defeat of art.

In *Utopia Parkway* Drexler's metamorphic impulse is at its most charming and sorrowing pitch. Bill, an artist very much like Joseph Cornell, the sainted master of boxed assemblage, is visited by Mildred, a dancer very much like those steel-muscled muses of the great choreographer, George Balanchine. The latter is metamorphosed into Mr. B, who's a barber as well as a choreographer, specializing in tonsorial styles like "the Blunt Iago. It insinuates everything and can create quite a stir." But art can only insinuate its own despair and stir up its own panic. "It is my job," says Mr. B, "to help nature along, to design a pattern that makes nature and art one." but he's talking as a barber, not as a choreographer, and his speech is the chatter of the magisters of the fashion world, who have largely replaced artists as the agents of meaningful metamorphosis. Poor old Bill is a creature of delicate pathos, telling Mildred she reminds him of "my bluebird of happiness, my teakettle and tiny cat playing with a pretty ball"—images from the Xanadu of keepsakes from which he fashions his dreams-in-a-box. This gossamer esthetic Bill explains by saying, "After a long detour by way of dreams, we learn to love reality a little better." But this world of art, a flanking action to evade the brutish force and steel the transcendent heart of reality, is smashed by an apparent CIA agent who accuses Mr. B of being a spy. "Every artist is a spy," says Mr. B. Drexler's resolution to this cubistic contretemps is a thing of crazy grace and sad sublimity, as Bill constructs a living collage from colliding beauties of this world, in which, as Mildred says, " . . .that death in the abstract is life."

Out of these dances, dirges, and drolleries emanating from the shadow-war in which art's adversaries are everything, including itself, Drexler makes high and sagacious comedy. She is a tough-minded poet and a total theatrician; these plays contain magical things, such as the opening of *Utopia Parkway*, in which Bill sits alone in his room suffused in "a shower of light (like brushed-out golden hair) that filters over him from an overhead skylight" while "Cage-ian music" sounds as Bill, with ancient exquisiteness, tunes himself into the evanescent emanations of art. The CIA man natters on about computers, but these plays make no easy polemics about technology destroying sensibility. Like her ancestor Alfred Jarry, Drexler evokes and investigates the internal contradictions of consciousness constantly subverted by the rough realities of culture and by its own guilt. In these witty and heartbreaking plays, she turns the shattered heroism of the artist into the masquerading humanity that heroism always concealed. She knows this moment is a violently vulgar one, but vulgarity and violence have their own dimensions of subtlety, and these plays are both subtle and hearty: they wisecrack and whisper as the accompanying music to their dance of life.

ROOM 17C

The bug in *Room 17C* should not be in bug costume; a well-worn brown suit will suffice. The actor should, in his movement and delivery of lines, project a bug persona, i.e., an affinity for the corners of the room—crawling, scurrying in a nervous manner, flattening out, creeping upon, hanging from, hiding. He is *not* to be cute, but must engage our compassion and encourage the audience's recognition that they, too, are vulnerable and at one time or another have been 'bugs' themselves. Perhaps a bug is someone who has given up one lifestyle for another; has chosen to retire from the 'rat race,' and therefore is regarded by others as the lowliest of the low, a bug. The bug is not sad; he accepts what he is. This frees his spirit. He does not have to be what he is not.

Linda has taken over her husband's destiny to be a successful salesman. Her life still is not her own. Her husband keeps calling her to check up on her. She has to harden herself. In some way she still is playing his 'masochistic' game. Whatever she does pains him. He threatens her with his suicide, but it is she who will die (in the line of duty, burned to a crisp with her sport's 'knock-em-dead' line).

With the bug Sammy Gregor, Linda begins to play, to relate irreverently and romantically to another creature: They open up to each other as strangers often do.

The situation is odd, is absurd, but should be played as realistically as possible since this will emphasize the absurdist element rather than detract from it. This play is *not* Kafka goes to Disneyland. (Note: The set also should be 'real.')

CHARACTERS

LINDA NORMAL	A traveling saleswoman
SAMMY GREGOR	A man-sized cockroach
JOEY NORMAL	Male in his early twenties; Linda's son

(A hotel room: Twin bed, dresser with mirror, chair, night table. There is a phone on night table.)

(A suitcase is open on the bed. There are women's clothes in suitcase.)

(There are two doors: one leading to the hall, the other to the bathroom.)

(The bathroom door opens. LINDA enters the room. She sits on the bed and dials the phone.)

LINDA: Hello, operator? I want to make a person-to-person call to Mr. Willy Normal. No, it is not a collect call. Charge it to my room. Thank you. *(She waits a few rings.)* Operator, operator . . . I'll try again later . . . . Thank you.

(She begins to unpack, carries a dress or two to the closet. Her back is to the bed.)

(A large, man-sized cockroach crawls from under the bed. At first only his head is visible.)

(LINDA hangs her dresses up. She turns around. At once she notices the cockroach observing her with his large, luminous eyes. She backs away, arms outstretched.)

LINDA: Oh!

COCKROACH: You seem to be a neat person. Ever leave food around?

LINDA: It talks! Wh-h, wh-h what do you want?

COCKROACH: I like it a few days old, at least. Brings out the flavor . . . . But I'll eat anything. My situation does not allow me to indulge a rather gourmet inclination.

LINDA: Either you crawl back into the woodwork or I call the front desk—they'll know what to do.

COCKROACH: That's a laugh. Exterminator comes once a month. That's it. Those of us who survive get carte blanche.

LINDA: You're loathsome.

COCKROACH: Loathsome and lonesome. I've learned to live with it. *(He crawls around the room, gathering speed. He jumps on bed and bounces.*) You'll like the bed. Lots of bounce. Once I got stuck on the ceiling. But then I plunked right down again. Lay on my back like this . . . . (*He lies on bed, feet waving in air.*) It's a dangerous position for me to be in; however, seeing things from above was worth it.

LINDA: How was it worth it?

COCKROACH: Changed my perspective. Running around the floor looking for shadows is an alienating experience. I despised myself. Every time the lights went on I ran for my life. You can't imagine the terror . . . but rising above it, ah-h! Changed my life. I've had my transcendental moment. (*He slowly edges toward* LINDA.)

LINDA: Don't come any closer, or I'll stomp you.

COCKROACH: No you won't. You don't want to have part of me stuck to your nice new shoes: bits of brown wing, cream filling . . . .

LINDA: Oh! I can smell you from here. I can smell every filthy place you've been.

COCKROACH: I think you're imagining it.

LINDA: No, I'm not imagining it. I have an exceptionally good sense of smell.

COCKROACH: Well, I suppose I do have a characteristic odor.

LINDA: It's offensive.

COCKROACH: I've been told by certain other transients that it reminds them of home.

LINDA: I pity you. (*She opens window and takes a deep breath.*)

COCKROACH: That's good.

LINDA: I don't really pity you. Why would I waste pity on your kind? Before long you'd be dependent on me.

COCKROACH: For what?

LINDA: You'd be all over me at night: a small bite here, a small bite there.

COCKROACH: Love nips don't last long; just enough pain to punctuate the pleasure.

LINDA: Keep me up itching all night long.

COCKROACH: You're right. Anything to make you notice me.

LINDA: You remind me of my husband Willy, always playing on my sympathy. He is, rather he *was*, a traveling salesman and a parasite, selling things to people that they didn't need: hair brushes made of hog's bristles, clothing brushes, toothbrushes, every kind of brush . . . to get them hooked he'd give them, absolutely free, a vegetable brush . . . . Well, he's fired now. Got a goldplated watch to commemorate his masochism. Who cares any more.

COCKROACH: Not you?

LINDA: Don't have time to cry. Not when you're on the road. Now it's me who attends to business: sales conferences, customer relations, filling quotas . . . afterwards, smoke-filled rooms, scotch and soda, running down the competition. It's better than waiting for things to change. They never will.

COCKROACH: Things *have* changed . . . for both of us.

LINDA: Don't link us together, please!

(*Cockroach moves toward* LINDA.)

LINDA: And stay where you are. This conversation is taking place only because I'm here, and you're here, and no one else is here.

COCKROACH: Speaking for the parasites of the world, what's so bad about being a parasite? All I want is a safe haven.

LINDA: And a free ride.

COCKROACH: In my former life I was a clerk. Brought home the paycheck: supported father, mother, sister . . . they

began to settle in . . . grew weak . . . lost weight . . . .
they became parasitic . . . . My ability to take care of things
took away their reason for being. Minute I changed,
ummm, took my present form and remained in my room
listening, just listening, they came to life again; they wanted
me to be dependent on them. You see before you a martyr.

LINDA: Are you telling me you *chose* to become a roach to
save your family? I think not! I think you're a dreamer who
grew his own shell to crawl into.

COCKROACH: Why I am the way I am hardly matters any
more, since I'm not changing back. This is it for me. Would
you excuse me for a few seconds?

LINDA: You going somewhere?

COCKROACH: To the bathroom pipes. How I love a tropical
climate! The pipes, the pipes, they sing to me of moist,
mother love. I was hatched from a nest of gritty black
specks, splattered according to nature's maternal time clock
upon a shiny brass pipe below a sink. Have you ever put
your ear to a pipe? You can hear the ocean that way. You
can even hear the sighs of baby alligators as they migrate, in
all innocence, to a watery grave.

(*He crawls to bathroom.* LINDA *slams door. She leans on it.*)

LINDA: You can stay in there forever! Don't try to soften me
with sad stories. I've heard 'em all. Where are the good old
happy stories? Where are the success stories? I want to
laugh. I want to laugh, dammit!

COCKROACH: You want to laugh? Oh, I'm sorry.

LINDA: Forget it.

COCKROACH: I'm ready to come out . . . . Hey, don't think
I'm trapped in here. Only human beings can be locked in. I
have access. I can go underground. I know the way back.

LINDA: And I can leave any time I want to. I can vacate the
premises . . . check out.

COCKROACH: Because of an insect? How unsophisticated! By the way, what's your name? I might have to beg for mercy, or curse my fate. Supplication has better results when one directs it to a specific deity, such as yourself.

LINDA: Linda Normal. Start begging.

COCKROACH: Sammy Gregor. Sammy's enough.

LINDA: You're living on borrowed time, Sammy.

COCKROACH: Say, Linda—what if you have to use the john?

LINDA: Let me worry about that.

COCKROACH: You'll have to stop leaning on the door.

LINDA: I'm not leaning on the door.

COCKROACH: They always lean on the door. I don't have to use a door to get in or out.

LINDA: Don't you?!

COCKROACH: You're the prisoner, Linda.

LINDA: (*She barricades the door with a piece of furniture.*) Why don't you shut up and listen to your pipes?

COCKROACH: Okay, but I have a tendency to sing along.

LINDA: Sing. Chirp. Whatever. Who cares. (*She dials phone.*) Hello, I want to make a person-to-person call to a Mr. William Normal. . . . Thank you.

COCKROACH: (*Sings—at first softly, but becomes louder. He is still in bathroom.*)

> BABY, I'M IN A STRANGE SITUATION
> CAN'T SAY I LIKE THIS NEW SENSATION
> YOU'VE GOT ME WHERE YOU WANT ME
> BEHIND CLOSED DOORS
> WHAT YOU GONNA DO WITH ME NOW?

LINDA: (*On phone.*) Willy? It's me, darling. Yes, I had a good trip down. You lonely already? Oh, don't be such a sad

sack, Willy, keep busy, get off your butt. So what if the
watch isn't digital? It's goldplated isn't it? No, I haven't
even unpacked yet. Met an irresistible stranger in the
elevator? Hardly! What? What'd you say?

COCKROACH: (*Sings.*)
> JUST WANT YOU TO
> KNOW ME
> TO SHOW ME
> THE WILD SIDE OF LOVE
> DON'T LEAVE ME
> RETRIEVE ME
> FROM LIFE'S OLD GARBAGE PILE

LINDA: No, nobody is here with me. It's the radio. Still have
'em in some hotels, you know. What program? Oh . . . .
Oldies But Goodies. Don't worry, I won't get into trouble.
I'm not you! I haven't hidden Mel Torme under the bed.
It's the *radio*. Believe me. Yes, darling, I forgive you for your
sexual transgressions. Yes, I know how it is on the road. You
were only looking for companionship, not for someone to
replace me. That's water under the bridge, Willy; forget it.
I've forgotten it. Where's your backbone, dammit? Sit up
straight, Willy, or no one'll know you're at the table.

COCKROACH: (*Sings.*)

> BABY, THIS IS THE PITS, DON'T DENY IT
> I'M 'LLOWED TO KNOCK IT, 'CAUSE I TRIED IT
> YOU'VE GOT ME WHERE YOU WANT ME
> RIGHT ON THE FLOOR
> WHAT YOU GONNA DO WITH ME NOW?

LINDA: I know you tried your best. So you were fired; why
suffer!? Enjoy life, Willy. I do. My spring line should knock
'em dead. They ain't never seen sportswear like this! . . .
Why do you want to go and ruin my trip? . . . No, no, no!
Don't kill yourself, darling! It'd be anti-climactic. You hear
me? You're not talking now. Willy? Willy? Of course I love
you. Here's a big kiss for you (*kissing sound*) . . . . (*She hangs
up.*) Damn! He wants me to give him a reason to live, on the

telephone! Hey, Sammy, how ya doin' in there? Why don't you climb down to the lobby and hide in a pile of newspaper?

(SAMMY *enters from bathroom.* LINDA *does not see him.*)

COCKROACH: Already been down.

(LINDA *whirls around.*)

LINDA: Oh! (*She backs up, runs into bathroom.*)

COCKROACH: There is no sanctuary for you, Linda.

LINDA: I don't want sanctuary. I want to pee.

(*While she is in the bathroom the cockroach goes through her luggage. He finds a pair of running trunks and puts them on. He runs in place.*)

COCKROACH: These running trunks are very comfortable.

LINDA: What running trunks?

COCKROACH: Found 'em in your luggage.

LINDA: Stop whatever you're doing till I come out.

COCKROACH: (*Observes himself in dresser mirror.*) I could model your line for you. Make you rich and famous.

LINDA: I'm not Walt Disney . . . . Be a sport, pal, disappear! (*She comes out of the bathroom.*)

COCKROACH: (*Gliding to window.*) Look out there, Linda. The world beckons. There's more to consider than you and me. There's street-corner religion. Pimps and prostitutes. The homeless. Everything deep-fried in hell. And at night, the crunch, crunch, crunch of rats and roaches on the prowl.

LINDA: I came here for two reasons: business and pleasure. What's out there doesn't mean beans to me. Besides, I've seen everything. I've seen you.

COCKROACH: And I disgust you, don't I.

LINDA: So far, yeah.

COCKROACH: (*Sits on bed.*) My sister wasn't disgusted by my transformation. She took care of me. Played her violin while I trembled in ecstasy. At the age of thirteen, when she became a woman, she pushed her violin into mother's lap. It slid to the floor, and broke. She went out the door to meet her friends. Didn't look back. After that, nobody paid any attention to me. It was as if I no longer existed. At night the door to my room was left open. In the half-light I could watch them all: sister bent over a book, mother intent on her sewing, father nodding half-asleep. . . . A tender family scene with their backs to me. Always their backs to me. I could have breathed my last, as the first broadening of light in the world outside the window entered my consciousness once more, but I decided to check into a hotel instead.

LINDA: Just like Willy. Too sensitive to fight back. I think you enjoy frightening people with that cockroach ugliness of yours. You wouldn't have it any other way.

COCKROACH: (*Removes running shorts and gets into bed.*) What other way can I have it?

LINDA: Get out of my bed! (*She picks up a shoe and hides it behind her back.*) I said get out! I will not let you turn this trip into a Japanese horror film.

COCKROACH: Get in.

LINDA: Get out.

COCKROACH: I saw your photograph.

LINDA: Photograph?

COCKROACH: In your suitcase; face down at first, swaddled in silk lingerie. Hidden by you.

LINDA: It was wrapped for safety. Glass breaks when luggage is handled roughly.

COCKROACH: You did hide it.

LINDA: Why would I do that? It is a perfectly ordinary photograph.

COCKROACH: Not to me. Your photograph is personal. Hardly a flight of flies above the butter dish.

LINDA: Personal? Yes it is personal; yet holding a pose goes beyond the personal into the painful. Family photographs reveal too much . . .dear Willy swooning at my feet, for instance. I can't remember whether the photographer suggested it, or whether passion had placed him there, underfoot. At any rate, he was more than willing to be there, his body flattened, his head at a tilt as if waiting for some final blow. In his brown suit, he resembled a bug, yes, a cockroach. Perhaps I *am* partial to cockroaches, Sammy, have always wanted them in the picture. But you, Sammy, are my first real cockroach. I smelled you—remember?—the minute I came into this room.

COCKROACH: (*Sings at* LINDA'S *feet.*)

JUST WANT YOU TO
USE ME
ABUSE ME
REFUSE WHAT I ASK
IGNORE ME
ABHORE ME
I'M EQUAL TO THE TASK

LINDA: You're so delicate, I might kill you by accident, forcing you to stay within an embrace beyond roach endurance; and what if you can't withstand the poetry of a magic moment?

COCKROACH: Ah, poetry, the deadly stranger in our midst. . . . Come to bed.

(LINDA *approaches. She hits him with the shoe. He shudders, then lies still.*)

LINDA: There's poetry in a shoe, too.

COCKROACH: I'm not dead yet.

LINDA: Why are you bugging me?

COCKROACH: I have my bug destiny to fulfill. I want to sit in your unshaved armpit, crawl between your thighs, investigate your glistening tongue, bask in your passionate hot breath.

(*Phones rings; * LINDA *answers.*)

LINDA: Yes? Willy? Is anything wrong? You can't find the instant coffee? Look in the cabinet over the sink. It should be there.

(*Cockroach crawls into her lap. She gives a small cry and brushes roach off.*)

Get off! Not you, Willy. A speck of dust. Flew in the window. It's so dirty here in New York. What? You've lost sympathy with me? I've made my bed, now I have to sleep in it? Why are you so mean to me? You're jealous, Willy. That must be it. You can't take it any more? No, you're not useless, Willy. Talk to Joey. He's a good son. He loves you. Of course he respects you. . . . Oh, I forgot to remind you to check the water heater. Pan has to be emptied. No, the hose does not lead directly to the gas line. Boy, do you sound depressed. Yes, I miss you. I began to miss you the minute I made my travel plans. You'd like this room, Willy, except for the roach infestation. . . . Say, keep your chin up, hon, I'll be home soon. What's a few days out of a marriage of twenty-five years? Yes, I love you, too. Always will. (*She hangs up.*)

LINDA: (*To Sammy.*) I've got to go downstairs now to sign in for my conference. If you're still here when I get back, you can kiss your feelers goodbye.

COCKROACH: I understand the logic of this particular situation.

LINDA: Do you?

COCKROACH: I am a utopian quester. You are utopia; however, I know when to back off.

LINDA: Let's hope so.

COCKROACH: (*Sings.*)

> BABY, I'M BEGGING YOU FOR A FAVOR
> CAN'T SAY I'VE EVER LICKED THIS FLAVOR
> YOU'VE GOT ME WHERE YOU WANT ME
> DENIED ME MY SWEETS
> WHAT YOU GONNA DO WITH ME NOW?

LINDA: For someone who revels in dung and bird droppings you have a romantic nature. Still, don't be here when I get back.

(*She exits. Cockroach goes to phone and imitates* LINDA'S *voice.*)

COCKROACH: Room service? This is Room 17C. I'd like to order some food. Two hamburgers, rare. Sauteed onions. A bottle of Moet-Chandon tres sec. And a plate of chocolate-covered mints. I'll be in the shower, so please leave the table outside the door. Thank you.

(*He hangs up. Goes into bathroom. Time passes. Knock on door. After a few minutes, Roach goes to door and wheels table of food in Examines food. Tastes it. Examines champagne label. Puts bottle back into ice bucket.*)

Life can be so pleasant! A roof over one's head, food on the table, and a beautiful adversary in the grand ballroom.

(LINDA *returns.*)

LINDA: Still here?

COCKROACH: I've taken the liberty of ordering a celebration feast.

LINDA: They take orders from a cockroach?

COCKROACH: From a voice on the phone.

LINDA: (*Examines the champagne.*) What's wrong with Perrier? It's a lot cheaper.

COCKROACH: The downtrodden need more than bread and water.

LINDA: Hamburgers! I love 'em. . . . Is this food rotten enough for you?

COCKROACH: Nothing's rotten enough for me, but this'll have to do.

LINDA: I'm really hungry, but please don't crawl over my food or I'll throw up.

COCKROACH: My table manners are impeccable, dear Linda. I haven't forgotten mother's linen tablecloths and silver . . . father's crystal goblets and precisely folded napkins.

(*They sit at table.*)

LINDA: (*While eating.*) Thing is, concerning Willy and my son Joey . . . They haven't gotten along since Joey walked in on Willy when he was with some woman, somewhere . . . Pass me the pickles . . . . Thanks . . . . Here, you take some, too . . . . Willy's always tried to help the kid; introduced him to the district manager of his firm . . . set the kid up with his own route. . . . Well, Joey was gung-ho to start, arrived a day early, and that's when he found out his dad wasn't one-hundred percent perfect. Talk about men putting women on a pedestal! Joey had his dad living on Mount Everest. Poor kid, thought he had to take sides, defend me; I couldn't have cared less.

COCKROACH: You didn't care?

LINDA: Nothing I could do about it. His life is his life. All he talked about was how his life was slipping through his fingers. I said Willy, the time to start worrying is when your fingers start slipping through your fingers. Oh, I was sorry for him: age creeping up, nothing to show for a lifetime of work. But I couldn't solve it for him. . . . More ketchup? . . . I'm a ketchup freak. Give me a prime steak and I'll smother it in ketchup. Ummmm. . . . What does the man want?

COCKROACH: Another chance, maybe.

LINDA: At what?

COCKROACH: Going backwards instead of forwards.

LINDA: Why would anyone want to be young?

COCKROACH: The young have a future.

LINDA: The young want us dead so they can take over. Willy understands that, but he can't bear the thought of it. He's taken out insurance for Joey. Says if he can't take care of him properly when he's alive, he'll look out for him after he's dead. He needs that boy's love more than anything in the world. . . .

COCKROACH: The sweetness and the sorrow. . . .Damn! I think there's ground bone in this hamburger—almost broke my mandible.

LINDA: You have no regrets? I mean about your transformation . . . the loss of teeth, a life sans eyelids, sans ears, sans all the basic equipment you once had as a human being.

COCKROACH: No.

LINDA: I have regrets. I've spent most of my life with a man who does not love life. . . . You, a bug, raise my spirits and make me feel that is it possible to be really happy. . . . You would not hang on to me. You have your life. I have mine. Did you say you knew the way back?

COCKROACH: I said I was a physical parasite.

LINDA: So you said. . . . Let's open the champagne.

(*Cockroach opens the champagne. He pours it. He smells the cork. he swishes champagne around in his mouth.*)

COCKROACH: Good, good; it is much better than vinegar. (*Glass raised.*) Cheers!

LINDA: (*Glass raised.*) Cheers!

(*They drink.*)

COCKROACH: (*Sings.*)

> BABY, I'M IN THE MOOD FOR A TANGO
> OR SHALL WE DANCE THE LIGHT FANDANGO?
> YOU'VE GOT ME WHERE YOU WANT ME
> SO I REPEAT
> WHAT YOU GONNA DO WITH ME NOW?

LINDA: Yes, let's dance. I'll close my eyes and pretend not to hear the urgent rustling of your crisp shell, the rush of wind as it tosses those useless wings of yours around me. . . .

COCKROACH: Have no fear.

(*He takes her in his arms. They dance.*)

Munch the painter, painted a woman dancing with death. He didn't trust women, but was irresistibly drawn to them. Strindberg, too.

LINDA: Oh, yes, victims of sexual dysfunction, both of them. Skeletons have no right to yearn for flesh. Not in their condition . . . yet. . . .

COCKROACH: Yet what used to be, echoes in their bones.

LINDA: They need blood. Where do they get it?

COCKROACH: The paint tube; the inkwell. Looks real enough.

LINDA: From the placenta, I think. Every man wants to be belly to belly with his past.

(*Dance ends.*)

COCKROACH: Come here.

LINDA: You have nothing to lose.

COCKROACH: Physical contact. Remember, I'm a physical parasite.

(LINDA *approaches the cockroach slowly. When she is near the bed he grabs her, and throws her down.*)

LINDA: Forgive me for believing there are creatures lower than myself. Let me go.

(*There is a knock on door.*)

JOEY: (*Voice from hall.*) Mom? Are you in there? It's Joey, Mom.

LINDA: Damn. It's my kid. Why the heck is he here? . . . Joey?

JOEY: It's me, Mom.

LINDA: I'll be right there. (*To cockroach.*) Hide—get under the bed.

COCKROACH: No.

LINDA: Please—if Joey sees us together he'll be traumatized.

JOEY: Mom?

LINDA: Coming.

COCKROACH: Let him in. You haven't done anything to be ashamed of.

(LINDA *opeans door. Joey enters. They embrace. He sees cockroach on bed.*)

JOEY: God! Who's the guy in the costume? . . .Oh, no. . . . You've been cheating on Dad. How could you do this to me!

LINDA: To you? What right do you have to come sneaking around here? I'm a grown woman with a life of my own.

COCKROACH: Name's Sammy Gregor. I'm a mutant. Anything else you want to know?

LINDA: He's a friend. That's all.

JOEY: He's a stranger. . . . He's stranger than that, too.

COCKROACH: I'm not a stranger. When I was smaller I lived in your house. You didn't notice me. I hugged the baseboards and slept wrapped in beds of dust.

JOEY: (*To* LINDA.) No wonder Dad turned to other women. You stepped all over him. And now this . . . this insect. . . . What does he have that Dad doesn't?

LINDA: Feelers! He has feelers. Looks aren't everything.

JOEY: Mother, you are the lowest of the low. You are below sea level. You are a reef that harbors poisonous fish and other prickly denizens. Where it is darkest, coldest, timeless, you find pleasure. You have no temperature of your own but take on the icy temperature of bone-chilling currents. You do not care where you drift, so long as there is movement. And you do not even notice that this movement is carrying you away from those who love you. Woman is a perilous craft, and crafty though she is, cannot avoid the rocks in her path, so ready is she to abandon herself to the elements . . . to wreck what has formerly had direction and buoyancy.

LINDA: I hadn't realized that I had raised a woman hater, Joey; and an excessively literary one to boot. Why don't you go commiserate with your admirable father? Time to renew old ties. You broke his heart. There's still time to mend it.

JOEY: I didn't hurt Dad, you did. That's why he wants to kill himself. He's all by himself, while you whore around with this night crawler!

LINDA: For what it's worth Joey, Mr. Gregor and I have not been intimate. We were just having some dinner together, and conversing on an elevated plane.

JOEY: Honest?

LINDA: Honest. Isn't that right, Mr. Gregor?

COCKROACH: Yes. Conversing on an elevated plane, not yet aloft.

JOEY: That's different. (*He goes to window.*) Hey. . . . Hey there's smoke coming out of the hotel. (*Sound of fire engines.*) Let's get out of here. . . .C'mon.

(*The three of them run for the door. They exit. Phone rings. Smoke billows into room.* LINDA *reappears. She answers the phone.*)

LINDA: Willy . . . Willy . . . Sneaky of you, Willy . . . (*Coughs*). . . . Sending Joey to spy on me. . . . (*Coughs*)

. . . Today is your last day on earth? . . . Funny, I feel that way too. . . .(*Coughs*) Remember to put out the pilot light on the heater and the stove. . . . Yes, the clothes dryer, too. . . . If the house blows up, where will Joey live? . . . (*Cough*) . . . And listen, Willy, I've never loved you. . . . You're as cold as yesterday's mashed potatoes. This evening I met someone, fell in love, and am about to die of smoke poisoning. . . . (*Coughs*) . . . Tell me, Willy, were all the lies worth it? . . . (*Cough*) . . . Goodbye. Willy. . . . (*She passes out on the bed.*)

(*Cockroach enters.*)

COCKROACH: Linda! Linda! Where are you? (*He finds her on the bed. He examines her to see if she is alive. She is not. He walks to stage front and addresses the audience.*)

COCKROACH: Life is surprisingly short. I cannot understand why Linda would have turned back to answer the telephone. Force of habit? Destiny? The irresistable distance from door to bed proved fatal. Linda has not survived. In death she lacks the livelier character of former times. I'd weep if I could. Take this dry rustling of my useless wings as a sign of sorrow. I am left. And I grieve. But I am always left. Or is it that I remain while others destroy themselves? I an insect, survive; I who crawl out of offal and debris. I, an insect, a vermin, the lowliest of the low, stay. I do not invent change; I adapt to the natural order of things. Even mushroom clouds cannot divert my way of life. My lifestyle is as old as the ocean. Of course I lack imagination. Lucky for me. Linda had imagination. Imagination can accomplish the end of the world. Life is long enough for that. Excuse me for blaming Linda; I tend to lump all human beings together. We do share the same planet. Long live earth and the creatures who live upon it. . . . And now, before I travel on, allow me to sing the popular roach anthem (*Sings*):

OH WOE IS ME
FOR MISERY
FOR BUGS OF LITTLE BRAIN

FOR PURPLE BRUISES INFAMY
AND LIFE'S UPROOTED PAIN
OH COCKROACH
OH COCKROACH
GOD HAS DISTASTE FOR THEE
YET HE DOES GOOD, AS WELL HE SHOULD
FOR ME, AND YOU, AND WE.

END OF PLAY

LOBBY

CHARACTERS

BLANCHE	An aging Southern belle (like Zelda Fitzgerald)
OSCAR	Oscar Wilde
TEDDY	A young addict
ESTRALITA	Teddy's friend (A young woman)
MR. ROSS	Hotel clerk/reception desk
ROBERT PEERLESS	Artist

Time: The present
Place: The lobby of a hotel similar to the Chelsea Hotel in NYC

(MR. ROSS *is behind lobby desk;* BLANCHE *is nervously pacing.*)

BLANCHE: Do they know how it started?

MR. ROSS: Smokin' in bed. Hole this big, in the mattress. Shoulda seen it.

BLANCHE: Who was it?

MR. ROSS: New guy. You don't know him.

BLANCHE: Is he . . . in the hospital?

MR. ROSS: Wherever. He's dead.

BLANCHE: Oh . . . (*She sits on the couch. Hopefully.*) Maybe he's not dead.

MR. ROSS: Tried to revive him right here in the lobby. He's dead, all right.

BLANCHE: I'm so very sorry.

MR. ROSS: Why?

BLANCHE: Why?

MR. ROSS: A complete stranger.

BLANCHE: Was he young?

MR. ROSS: What difference does his age make? He's gone.

BLANCHE: Did it make any difference when he was here?

MR. ROSS: It doesn't make any difference about any of us, Blanche. When we go it's as if we never were here. That's the sad part.

BLANCHE: Not the only sad part; what about me? I'm here but, so what, I might as well be dead.

MR. ROSS: Now don't let's get on that again. I can name at least two tenants who think the world of you: that cute little Estralita with the junky boyfriend, and Mr. Wilde.

BLANCHE: An illustrious choir of praise, indeed.

MR. ROSS: Hey, you like art, right?

BLANCHE: Love it, Mr. Ross. I make it my business to visit the Metropolitan Museum of Art at least once a month. How else could I wander through the centuries, experiencing the wonder of creation as it stands upon a pedestal, or hangs upon the wall?

MR. ROSS: But you don't own any.

BLANCHE: True, true; I have not yet begun my collection. Finances do not allow me to indulge in such luxuries.

MR. ROSS: I've got something for you. Don't have to take it if you don't like it. (*He brings a canvas out from behind his desk.*) I prefer nudes myself. . . . So what do you think? (*Indicating the landscape painting.*)

BLANCHE: Yes, yes . . . landscapes do appeal to me. I was brought up on the land, Mr. Ross. And as for your nudes, they're here, behind the trees, and swimming underwater in this lake . . . every dark cloud that obscures the moon, if you look very carefully, is actually an unmoored form floating in space.

MR. ROSS: If you want it, take it now before I call Salvation Army to take it away.

BLANCHE: Where did you get it? I'd like to meet the artist; offer my congratulations.

MR. ROSS: The guy who died today, he did it. I went into his room; could only save this.

BLANCHE: (*Sadly.*) Oh my, my, my, my, my what a shame. Are you sure he has no next of kin who'd want it? It's so beautiful: the sensitivity is authentic . . . unmistakable. Ever hear of Albert Pinkham Ryder?

MR. ROSS: No. Who's he?

BLANCHE: Another painter. American. He knew his blacks, browns, and gold. Put on coat after coat of shellac: adding sheen, patina, and mystery to his work. . . . Cracked eventually.

MR. ROSS: Ryder or his paintings?

BLANCHE: Both, no doubt . . . (*Examines the painting closely.*) It's signed . . . If I make it out correctly it's Robert Peerless . . . Peerless, yes that's it. Am I right?

MR. ROSS: Right. Shy guy, kept to himself.

BLANCHE: A transient; you said so yourself. Didn't have time to make friends.

MR. ROSS: Didn't want to. Firemen said he was out safe, but then ran back in again. Wanted to die.

BLANCHE: Firemen see so much tragedy, they have to invent a romantic aspect. Was he terribly burned?

MR. ROSS: Charcoal broiled, except for his eyes: clear blue to the end, till I closed his eyelids for him.

BLANCHE: You touched him? Mr. Ross, excuse me if I weep.

MR. ROSS: I'll carry the painting up to your room. Come on, lobby's no place to cry, Blanche. (*Gives her his handkerchief.*)

BLANCHE: Thank you . . . I'm okay . . . Besides, the smoke is still wafting about on the third floor. Can hardly breathe up there. Even the mice, who were quite comfortable in the wall under the sink, have been seen racing for the exits.

(OSCAR *enters. His hand is to his head.*)

OSCAR: (*Bows to each person he greets.*) Blanche . . . Mr. Ross . . . Oh, this ear has me reeling. I can't imagine what is bothering it; the things it hears, or some unheard-of malady.

MR. ROSS: You should go to the emergency room.

OSCAR: All of life is an emergency room, dear Ross, but I only care to see doctors when I am in perfect health; then they comfort one, but when one is ill they are most depressing.

BLANCHE: I'll go with you if you'd like.

OSCAR: What I'd like is a pack of gold-tipped cigarettes, half a liter of the best Chandon served in a crystal carafe, and an evening's dalliance with that fifteen-year-old who was with us in the elevator the night it got stuck.

MR. ROSS: Couldn't locate your wallet the next day. I think that kid picked your pocket.

OSCAR: That sensational creature wouldn't know how to pick his own nose.

MR. ROSS: Sure.

OSCAR: But, since you've brought the subject of money up, Ross, I wonder if I could borrow a small sum from you; my check is late, and I must visit the welfare office once again. I believe they have me coming and going so often because I amuse them.

MR. ROSS: How small a sum?

OSCAR: Anything you can spare . . . I promise to put it to good use.

MR. ROSS: (*Examines a roll of bills.*) Take ten . . . you need more, let me know.

OSCAR: Thank you, sir, from the bottom of my heart. . . . I'll pay you back as soon as I can.

MR. ROSS: I don't lend money, Mr. Wilde, I give it. That way I don't have to worry about getting it back. . . . Maybe you can use this coupon. . . . Two for the Price of One at Burger King with a small Coke thrown in.

OSCAR: (*Takes the coupon.*) I shall certainly use it, Mr. Ross. (*To* BLANCHE.) Blanche, would you care to join me?

BLANCHE: No thank you, I've already dined (*Obviously lying.*) at the marvelous Spanish restaurant next door.

MR. ROSS: How come you brought a bag of empty cat tins down to the basement? You don't have any cats.

BLANCHE: That's true, not in my room . . .the little darlings who inhabit the lower regions of this establishment need to be fed, too. . . . Although the Cheshire cat is too ephemeral for nine lives. . . . He lives forever, that's why he's smiling.

MR. ROSS: If I was you I'd stop going to the basement alone. You're tempting fate.

BLANCHE: I tempt more than fate, Mr. Ross. Young men are irresistibly drawn to me. In fact I'm expecting a proposal through the mail this very week. Is there anything for me in my box?

MR. ROSS: (*Looks.*) Nothing. Check with me tomorrow.

OSCAR: (*To* BLANCHE.) Still time to change your mind, Blanche. I'd welcome your company.

BLANCHE: No, I'm really not hungry, but I'll wait for you here in the lobby where I can contemplate this work of art. What do you think of it, Mr. Wilde?

OSCAR: (*Examining the painting.*) It is as silent as Whistler's songs on stone, and as nocturnal as his nocturnes in blue and gold . . . Really strong work. Who is the artist? I hope he will not accuse me of having the courage of the opinions of others.

BLANCHE: The artist is no longer with us. He died in this morning's fire.

OSCAR: Ah-h . . . then he is forever denied the privilege of living a life unworthy of an artist. Tant pis!

BLANCHE: This is all there will be. (*She dabs at her eyes.*)

OSCAR: (*Recites*):
   AND ALIEN TEARS WILL FILL FOR HIM
   PITY'S LONG BROKEN URN
   FOR HIS MOURNERS WILL BE OUTCASTS
   AND OUTCASTS ALWAYS MOURN.
(*He turns to leave.*)

BLANCHE: Oscar, if you happen to leave half a sesame bun on your plate, save it for me. I'm an inveterate midnight snacker; don't expect I'll change.

(OSCAR *nods in acquiescence; he exits.*)

BLANCHE: Oscar looks feverish: his eyes are glassy, his color too high, and when he was near me I could smell his breath.

(*A young male junky,* TEDDY, *enters with his girlfriend,* ESTRALITA. TEDDY *makes it halfway across lobby, stops, and goes into a bent-over position. He freezes in this (nodding out) position.*)

MR. ROSS: UH-oh.

ESTRALITA: (*To* TEDDY.) C'mon, Teddy. (*Tries to stand him up.*) C'mon. What you want anyway. You wanna go? You wanna stay?

MR. ROSS: (*To* ESTRALITA.) Your mamma's been looking for you.

ESTRALITA: Yeah?

MR. ROSS: She's been down here askin'.

ESTRALITA: Great. So she made it to the lobby: bought her smokes, made her calls; now she's back in bed. What the hell do I care.

MR. ROSS: Don't bite *my* head off.

ESTRALITA: (*To* TEDDY.) You comin'? Hey man, get yourself together!

TEDDY: Yeah . . . well, yeah . . .dynamite.

(TEDDY *continues to nod out, in bent but standing position.* ESTRALITA *sits next to* BLANCHE *on couch.*)

ESTRALITA: (*To* BLANCHE; *studies what* BLANCHE *is wearing.*) You make that yourself? (*Amused.*) It's *ug-lee*!

BLANCHE: We originals do have a difficult time of it.

ESTRALITA: Find it in the garbage?

BLANCHE: My dear, the best things in life are free, but what one does with them is where the originality comes in.

ESTRALITA: Now look at Teddy: he knows how to dress, but

he's lost interest. I got him them jeans and cowboy shirt . . . them boots . . . he just don't care.

BLANCHE: How can he, in that condition.

ESTRALITA: He could. He really could. Teddy's got the -makings of a super finesse dude. One day, well maybe not too soon I admit, he'll be okay. You see how he's movin', like he's bein' pulled one way then the other? He's hooked, that's why: like a half-asleep fish . . . one way, then the other. He don't jerk around, try to rip the hook out. He's afraid. Don't wanna get hurt. I'm tryin' to help him ease it out, so's he don't bleed . . . but you know what? Sometimes I think that hook's in too deep.

BLANCHE: Can't you get him into a program? Odyssey House? Phoenix House? Somewhere.

ESTRALITA: Can't. You gotta come to them with nothin' in your blood, show you really want to be clean. But I could be wrong. Anyway, Teddy likes things the way they are—shitty. (*To* TEDDY.) You ready to make your move Mr. T? Hey, who made you into a statue? (*Approaches* TEDDY; *helps him.*) Here we go . . .

(TEDDY *leans on* ESTRALITA. *They make their way to the elevator.*)

BLANCHE: What floor you on?

ESTRALITA: Ten. Why?

BLANCHE: The air is better up there. The fire was confined to the lower floors.

ESTRALITA: What fire?

MR. ROSS: Second floor front. You missed the excitement.

ESTRALITA: Next time.

(MR. ROSS *comes out from behind the desk to help* ESTRALITA *walk* TEDDY *to the elevator.*)

ESTRALITA: Thanks, man.

MR. ROSS: Put the load on granny.

(ESTRALITA *and* TEDDY *enter elevator.* MR. ROSS *returns to his place behind lobby desk.*)

MR. ROSS: More and more. Younger and younger. Nothin' to do and nowhere to go. Tough times, Blanche.

BLANCHE: That's true.

(OSCAR *enters.*)

OSCAR: One thing strikes me forcibly as I enter these portals: the smell of charcoal and burnt plastic; it has sanctified the usual stench and prepared me for my final descent into hell.

BLANCHE: Every step I take prepares me for that.

OSCAR: (*Gives* BLANCHE *a bag of food.*) Your sesame bun, madame, plus a crisp slice of pickle, a greasy pat of chopped meat, a dollop of ketchup, and a pungent, pearly, full moon of onion.

BLANCHE: Well, I'll just have to eat it . . . to please you. (*Begins to eat.*) Ummmm, it is delicious . . . not quite like the old days . . . picnics under the weeping willows: ham, black-eyed peas, corn bread and red-eye gravy. . . . Some days I had to take refuge in my bath, soaking for hours in the hot soapy water.

OSCAR: I, too, adore the south . . . of France. The Riviera, Nice, . . . beautiful people, beautiful flowers. I was never without a green carnation pinned to the lapel of my jacket . . . but in Italy, ah, there beauty comes running to meet one. At Nice I knew three lads like bronzes, quite perfect in form. English lads are chryselephantine, Swiss people are carved out of wood with a rough knife, most of them; the others are carved out of turnips . . . There were lovely walks by the lake, through the grounds of others: but I am a born trespasser.

BLANCHE: You know what happens to trespassers when they're caught.

OSCAR: Too well . . . once I trespassed upon a rose—forced it open with the sweet breath of desire . . . one by one its petals fell at my feet. . . . The thorns have not been removed yet.

BLANCHE: Yes, one goes to the hospital for a simple thing such as the removal of a thorn, but then complications set in and one is not allowed to leave. . . .There's too much mayonnaise on this bun.

OSCAR: I could have asked them to hold the mayo, madame, if I had known of your preference.

BLANCHE: Preference yes . . . I hadn't known of my young husband's preference. . . . When I confronted him with the sexual mayonnaise, so to speak, he left the dance, and shot himself on the veranda, adding ketchup to his ghastly sweetbreads.

OSCAR: To remember how we suffered in the past is necessary for our identity.

BLANCHE: There is suffering, and then there is suffering.

OSCAR: Ah, yes, the refinements of suffering. . . . It is better not to be different than one's fellows.

BLANCHE: It must be worse for you than for me.

OSCAR: No, it's the same for all of us. Jail taught me that. Treatment according to the law. Cruelties bestowed on one by otherwise kind people who were obeying the rules. Children and madmen had the worst of it. Already isolated from society by their tender age, by the odd embroideries of mental illness, they could not understand society's punishments: coarse Indian gruel and water for supper, birch rod beatings, the dim, locked cells smelling of diarrhea and slop.

BLANCHE: My confinement to a strait-jacket made me itch. I hugged myself, but not for comfort. After a while the ache went away; I remained flattened against myself. (*She stands, and flings the sandwich bag. It barely misses* MR. ROSS.) I want to inflate. I want to float above the parade. To be the parade.

(*She sits again.*) I have a great weight on my chest, Mr. Wilde. Do you think it will go away? Will I ever be light again?

OSCAR: Light as a feather, Blanche. You'll have a choice: tickle or float.

BLANCHE: Yes. Yes. . . . an egret feather, or an ostrich feather . . . so decorative. I love beautiful things. . . . The day I was released from the sanitorium my sister came to get me. She brought me things I had been denied inside: a necklace to choke myself with, furs to smother in, a beaded gown to trip over, and rings so heavy I could not lift my hands.

(OSCAR *and* BLANCHE *act out the sister scene outside the sanitorium.*)

OSCAR: (*As* BLANCHE'S *sister.*) You're looking well.

BLANCHE: Am I?

OSCAR: Better than before. The rest has done you good.

BLANCHE: Has it?

OSCAR: I've bought you a ticket to New York City. You can look out the bus window, it'll amuse you. Don't talk to strangers. The world's full of crazy people.

BLANCHE: I'm one of them.

OSCAR: I love you, Blanche.

(*They embrace.*)

BLANCHE: I love you, too.

BLANCHE: (*End of sister enactment.*) She does love me, wherever she and Stanley are. But you see, she really does not understand me: she let them take me away, she stayed with Stanley, she blamed me for the rape! At any rate, the streetcar has been renamed: Despair.

OSCAR: The past is not irrevocable.

BLANCHE: The past is all there is.

OSCAR: It is part of one's life, true, but there is more to come.

BLANCHE: That's what I was afraid of.

OSCAR: One must find a way to detach oneself from the accidents of life. That is difficult to do in this hotel. It has cramped my style . . . lack of money, to put it bluntly, has entailed in me a chastity and sobriety that is foreign to my nature.

BLANCHE: But don't you find that you have more time to write now, Mr. Wilde?

OSCAR: Time has nothing to do with creative output, Blanche. Writing is not piecework, it is piecemeal. However, just this morning I attempted a masterpiece:

(MR. ROSS *stands on desk; he becomes Christ.* BLANCHE *kneels at his feet; she becomes a mourning Mary.*)

> CHRIST, DOST THOU LIVE INDEED? OR ARE THY BONES
> STILL STRAITENED IN THEIR ROCK-HEWN SEPULCHRE?
> AND WAS THY RISING ONLY DREAMED BY HER
> WHOSE LOVE OF THEE FOR ALL HER SIN ATONES
> FOR HERE THE AIR IS HORRID WITH MEN'S GROANS,
> THE PRIESTS WHO CALL UPON THY NAME ARE SLAIN,
> DOES THOU NOT HEAR THE BITTER WAIL OF PAIN
> FROM THOSE WHOSE CHILDREN LIE UPON THE STONES?
> COME DOWN, O SON OF GOD! INCESTUOUS GLOOM
> CURTAINS THE LAND, AND THROUGH THE STARLESS NIGHT

OVER THEY CROSS A CRESCENT MOON I
 SEE!
IF THOU IN VERY TRUTH DIDST BURST THE
 TOMB
COME DOWN, O SON OF MAN! AND SHOW
 THY MIGHT,
LEST MAHOMET BE CROWNED INSTEAD OF
 THEE!

(*End of enactment.*)

OSCAR: I openly acknowledge my debt to Milton, who inspired me.

BLANCHE: Thank you, Oscar.

(ESTRALITA *enters from the elevator.*)

ESTRALITA: (*Agitated.*) Mr. Ross. It's Teddy. He's not moving. I can't get him to move. . . .

MR. ROSS: I'll call 911, you get back upstairs . . .

ESTRALITA: I'm getting out, Mr. Ross . . . I have to. . . . They find the drugs in him, they'll want to talk to me about it. . . . Oh, shit!

MR. ROSS: Is he in the room with your mother?

ESTRALITA: Naw. In his own room. In his own bed. At least that. He was shivering, so I covered him. Then he stopped shivering. (*She exits out the street door.*)

MR. ROSS: Hello, yes, this is an emergency. . . . The address is . . .

(*Blackout, then lights up: Lobby, some time later.* OSCAR, BLANCHE, *and* MR. ROSS *in lobby.* OSCAR *seated on couch.*)

MR. ROSS: Just a matter of time. Everything's a matter of time. Tick-tock, tick-tock, then nothing. I'm all for faceless clocks.

BLANCHE: I'm for faceless people. Once a face becomes familiar, I hate to see it change. Death does that: it immobilizes expression . . . it changes the temperature, too . . . I didn't know what cold as marble meant until I kissed my father's forehead as he lay in his coffin. I wasn't ready for it; his flesh was hard against my lips and the icy cold shocked me. . . . I've got to go out for a walk, Mr. Ross. . . . I've got to be alone.

MR. ROSS: We'll be here when you get back. Take care now.

BLANCHE: Nothing can happen to me, my friend; there is holy intervention for some of us poor lost lambs.

MR. ROSS: Don't depend on it.

BLANCHE: Oh, but I've always depended upon the kindness of a benevolent creator.

(OSCAR *begins to rise from the couch.*)

OSCAR: I'll see you to the door.

BLANCHE: Don't bother to get up, Mr. Wilde, I can manage by myself. (*She exits.*)

MR. ROSS: (*Shakes his head.*) There she goes. One excuse or another, every night.

OSCAR: Where to?

MR. ROSS: Out to sell tit for tipple. Hell, you know that. Welfare doesn't hand out stamps for Thunderbird wine.

OSCAR: A pity, Mr. Ross . . . and yet, I still believe that this is the best of all possible worlds. (*Hand to forehead.*) I don't feel well at all. Do you mind if I lie down for a while? I assure you I won't be taken for a cushion. (*He lies down.*)

MR. ROSS: Why don't you walk over to St. Vincent's? . . . See what's wrong.

OSCAR: Mr. Ross, did you know that all trials are trials for one's life, just as all sentences are death sentences?

MR. ROSS: Not the sentences you write, Mr. Wilde.

OSCAR: Yes, all, all. And with my ability to write death sentences, I have not spared myself . . . however, the prose itself is deathless.

MR. ROSS: You should take it easy . . . I have some aspirin. . . .

OSCAR: Take it easy? That's impossible for me, Mr. Ross. I must wander round and round within the circle of my personality. Must keep moving. Vultures keep their distance when there is movement.

MR. ROSS: Oscar, don't you want to get well and do what you used to do?

OSCAR: An artist never does the same thing twice . . . ou bien c'est qu'il n'avait pas reussi. Ma vie d'avant la prison a été aussi reussi que possible. Maintenant c'est une chose achevée. Yet perhaps all is not lost. . . . If I could produce only one beautiful work of art I could rob malice of its venom and cowardice of its sneer . . . pluck out the tongue of scorn by the roots. . . .

MR. ROSS: Sure . . .

OSCAR: Not sure! I am unable to put forth a sustained effort . . . that ridiculous poem I recited before, was written in my youth. Le Roi de la vie has been robbed of his throne and lives a life of humiliation and pain. . . . Ohhhh, this ear!

MR. ROSS: Let me call you a cab . . . I'll pay.

OSCAR: As you wish.

MR. ROSS: (*Dials phone.*) Hello? Yes, I'd like a cab, soon as you can make it. . . . Hotel New York, twenty-third between ninth and tenth. . . . Good. . . . Passenger will be in the lobby, name is Wilde. (*Hangs up.*)

OSCAR: If you think I'm dying beyond my means, don't! When I die it will be with all the means at my command.

MR. ROSS: Who said anything about dying?

OSCAR: Mr. Ross, you didn't have to. . . . Oh, and by the way, don't let anyone into my room while I'm gone. . . . My cameras are irreplaceable, and my photographs of no interest to anyone but myself.

MR. ROSS: Naturally; I'll double lock the door. Everything'll be just the way you left it when you come back.

OSCAR: Not everything; the fields of lily and iris will have turned to dung, the entire quagmire beneath my feet not only poisoned, but ugly.

MR. ROSS: I'll find you a new carpet with a different design.

OSCAR: Dear Ross, if you knew me at all, you'd know that I above all others understand the importance of being earnest. When I speak of dung, I speak of it profoundly. They say that whatever I touch, I decorate . . . yet there is nothing I can do with dung. Art is the supreme reality, and life is already en plein de merde!

(*Sound of horn honking.*)

MR. ROSS: Think that's your cab, Oscar. I'll have a look. (*He goes to door, looks out.*)

MR. ROSS: Yup. . . . Here, I'll give you a hand.

(*He walks* OSCAR *to door.* OSCAR *exits.* MR. ROSS *stands in lobby momentarily, undecided as to his next move.*)

MR. ROSS: Better go up and lock that door.

(*He gets keys from a pegboard. He exits by way of the elevator.* BLANCHE *enters.*)

BLANCHE: So hot in here. (*She removes her jacket and tosses it on the couch. She observes the painting that is still leaning against the desk.*)

BLANCHE: Art for art's sake. That's what it is.

(ROBERT PEERLESS *enters. He is wearing burned clothing.*)

ROBERT PEERLESS: I'd like to do your portrait.

BLANCHE: (*Startled; she turns around to face him.*) You must be. . . . You must be. . . .

ROBERT PEERLESS: I should *be* alive. I'm Robert Peerless. The guy who painted that imitation of an imitation. It wasn't even good enough to get into the Village art show.

BLANCHE: You're *too* good. Nothing but junk down there.

ROBERT PEERLESS: So what do you say? C'n I paint you?

BLANCHE: I'd be honored.

ROBERT PEERLESS: Nude from the waist up.

BLANCHE: Anything for the artist. . . . (*She disrobes.*) I like my breasts. Do you?

ROBERT PEERLESS: I'll know after I've painted them. (*He paints as if there is a canvas.*)

BLANCHE: (*Indicating left breast.*) This breast wanted to nurse a child. (*Indicating right breast.*) And this breast thought it could conquer the world if the right man rested his head against it. (*Indicating the left breast.*) This breast tried to point the way but got lost itself. (*Indicating right breast.*) And this breast had to be flattened so I could draw the bow. (*Indicating left breast.*) This breast could sing up a storm (*Indicating the right breast.*) And this breast could keep a secret.

ROBERT PEERLESS: It's done. . . . My best work to date. . . .

BLANCHE: Let me see.

ROBERT PEERLESS: Sorry. You can't see it. . . . Unless you want to join me on the way out.

BLANCHE: I've just been out.

ROBERT PEERLESS: You haven't been *way* out.

BLANCHE: No, but I've been very, very far in . . . almost didn't come back.

ROBERT PEERLESS: Why?

BLANCHE: Why?

ROBERT PEERLESS: Never mind. So long, Blanche, and thanks for being my last and only collector.

BLANCHE: I know talent when I see it.

ROBERT PEERLESS: (*Starts to exit.*) I believe you, Blanche.

BLANCHE: Wait! I must ask you . . .

ROBERT PEERLESS: Yes?

BLANCHE: Were you safe, and then did you run back into the fire?

ROBERT PEERLESS: Didn't get the chance, Blanche. Never moved a muscle.

BLANCHE: Then it was a cruel lie! . . . Some people would like to believe that all artists, true artists, live tragic lives and die tragic deaths . . . but you wanted to live; you had everything to live for. . . . We could have been lovers. Could have been, could have been. . . . I'm so lonely . . . so very lonely, Robert.

(ROBERT PEERLESS *exits.*)

Brrr, it's cold in here. (*She puts her clothes on. She picks up canvas, carries it a bit unsteadily to elevator.*)

MR. ROSS: (*He exits from elevator, holds door for* BLANCHE.) How was it out, Blanche?

BLANCHE: Cold, Mr. Ross.

(*She exits into elevator.* MR. ROSS *returns to his place behind the desk. The switchboard buzzes, he answers.*)

MR. ROSS: Yes, Mr. Douglas. No, Mr. Douglas, Mr. Wilde did not leave a message for you, unless, let's see, there might be something in your box. (*He looks into mail compartment behind desk.*) There is a letter for you . . . I'll be here all night, yes, you can get it when you come in. . . . No, I'm not allowed to admit you to his room. He did not say anything about entrusting you with his cameras. . . . Look, Bosie, I do have a message for you: Mr. Wilde is in the emergency room at St. Vincent's Hospital. Why don't you talk to him there. . . . You have a previous engagement? . . . So does he. . . .(*Hangs up.*) So do we all.

(*Lights dim to black.*)

END OF PLAY

UTOPIA PARKWAY

CHARACTERS

BILL	An artist
MAN	A CIA agent
MILDRED	A ballet dancer
MR. B	A Barber/Choreographer (black)
RABBIT	A strange friend of Bill's

Time: The present
Place: Bill's studio/home

(BILL: *A thin man with a gaunt face, bald at top of head, gray hair bristling at sides of head; he is wearing a royal purple shirt. Beside him is a table covered with a vivid pink oilcloth. At his feet is a blue cloth tote bag. He is seated on a wooden chair with wide armrests. His eyes are closed—his right arm up, the hand gently cupped to his ear. He is concentrating.*)

(*The room is dim except for a shower of light (like brushed out golden hair) that filters over him from an overhead skylight.*)

BILL: It's always been this way, the . . .

(*We hear cage-ian music, serial music with minute adjustments of rhythm and notes.*)

BILL: Always been this way, the. . . . (*Music continues.*)

BILL: Been this way, the. . . . (*Music continues.*)

BILL: This way, the. . . . (*Music continues.*)

BILL: Way, the. . . . (*Music continues.*)

BILL: The. . . .

BILL: To talk about what I do not accomplish, is to talk, instead of working. The pattern is a wearisome affair. . . . It is a slow day.

(*Music begins. Music sneaks into melody of* The Seven Deadly Sins (*Weill*). MILDRED *enters, dancing.*)

BILL: Hello.

MILDRED: Hello yourself.

BILL: You are familiar. . . .The familiar surprises me every time.

MILDRED: Every time?

BILL: It's always been this way, the . . .

MILDRED: Are you going to finish the sentence? I'm willing to wait.

BILL: (*Shrugs.*) Always been this way. . . .

MAN: Never mind. I'd rather dance. Remember when I performed *The Seven Deadly Sins*? During the glutton section, Mr. B asked me to do some Pilates exercises; so I put my foot, like this, behind my head, and did two foot circles, corresponding to a circular part in the music. It was so ridiculous, so obvious that it got laughs.

BILL: I didn't see you . . . I wonder what I was doing at that time? Where I might have been?

MILDRED: When I dove through the silver foil, my partner was back there waiting to catch me; someone else watching through a peephole said, "Here she comes!" (MILDRED *lands on Bill's lap.*)

BILL: Nobody warned me. . . . You're so beautiful. (*He examines her face.*)

MILDRED: My face is reconstructed . . . a kind of death. When things are bad, I long for an operation . . . punishment in the abstract. Abstracted is one of my favorite words.

BILL: Have you never looked out the window of a bus as it goes down Main Street towards La Guardia Airport?

MILDRED: Yes, in an abstracted sort of way. I didn't see a thing.

BILL: There was a pink cloud in a field of blue, framed by the window. The cloud disintegrated.

MILDRED: I've been pink, and I've been blue. Pink is better.

BILL: Only when used properly . . . the juxtaposition of color. . . . It's always been this way . . . the. . . . Are you married?

MILDRED: (*Gets off* BILL'S *lap.*) Six weeks after I was married I left Mr. X.

BILL: The cloud was a rosy color: somewhere between dark apple and Autumn leaf red. . . . After Mr. X was there a Mr. Y?

MILDRED: There was a Dr. Z, Mr. X's speed doctor. He used to inject right into the vein. If the subject was a woman, he'd place her feet against his crotch as he injected her. Afterwards, I traveled a million miles an hour, but I couldn't catch up with Mr. X, my husband.

BILL: Regarding the cloud. It has been integrated into a collage that reminds me strongly of the collage work of Schwitters. His work is highly abstract, yet he employs easily recognizable material.

MILDRED: Do I seem highly abstracted to you?

BILL: Is the Chinese quince tree abstract? Are the robins, squirrels, starlings, and all strutting birds abstract?

MILDRED: My stretch marks are not abstract. My first child was not abstract. When Seven Deadly Sins was to go back, I said I couldn't do it. Later I had an operation to improve the way my stomach looked . . . ninety-nine stitches. The doctor cut too deeply on one side and my upper thigh went numb. That delayed me for a season or two.

BILL: Never mind. I don't mind. You have beautiful feet.

MILDRED: When I was ten, a doctor discovered I had flat feet. (*She demonstrates a flat-footed walk.*)

BILL: Manet painted a pair of flat feet beside a red fan, and then he painted a bouquet of violets over the feet. (*He gets a picture postcard of the Manet violets and fan.*) Here, take it.

MILDRED: I've always preferred flowers to ice-cream, drugs, and men. . . . Mr. X is trying to blackmail me with hundred dollar bills. He makes bouquets out of them. He's hardly a florist. When I reject his offering, he threatens to kill himself. He does that a lot.

BILL: After a long detour by way of dreams, we learn to love reality a little better.

MILDRED: I hate it! I hate it! A married man called me recently. He made a dinner date with me. Should I keep it? I love to eat, but married men don't interest me.

BILL: Send him a telegram. It's more definite than a telephone call.

MILDRED: Good idea. I'll send it to him, and to her, as if he had intended to include her. She doesn't know what he's up to. . . . I'll say: Dear so and so, and Dear so and so, I do want to stay in touch but have suddenly decided to take a vacation for one month starting today in another hemisphere which will have a different season. Highest regards from Mildred.

BILL: I perceive a thread of continuity . . . your movement from one man to another like scenes in an animated film. . . . Even our lives overlap dear Mildred, for you belong in my work: I see you in the landscapes, cloudscapes, and night skies . . . you are my bluebird of happiness, you are my tea-kettle and tiny cat playing with a pretty ball.

MILDRED: I expected you to talk like that: like an artist, and I knew you'd need a haircut, so I asked Mr. B the barber/choreographer to meet me here. He's the best. He'll know how to shape your head.

(*One clear bell note sounds. Mr. B enters.*)

MR. B: (*Takes scissors and clipper out of an attaché case. Indicating the scissors.*) The point is crucial. The blades must be sharp. The screw tightened just enough. I respect my tools. (*To* BILL.) You're the customer?

BILL: Sometimes I sell. Sometimes I buy. Sometimes I just let it go too far. I'm ready for a haircut.

MR. B: Good. Good. I wouldn't have wanted to come this far without giving you a trimming.

BILL: Mildred tells me that you are also a choreographer.

MR. B: True, but one needs something else to fall back on. Another trade. Surgery would have been too difficult, so I entered the Academy of Tonsorial Snip Snip. . . . Sit up straight, please. . . . Don't lean back.

BILL: Just take some off the sides.

MILDRED: Mr. B, thank you for making me a dancer.

MR. B: Mildred dear, a dancer is never finished. (*Begins the haircut.*) Like a haircut, the dancer must be done over and over again: balanced, trimmed, styled, tamed . . . choreographed hair by hair so that one does not point north and the other south. The head is a stage upon which every tiny dancer takes root, yet moves. It is a harmony of placement. It is my job to help nature along, to design a pattern that makes nature and art one.

MILDRED: What power and eloquence you have, Mr. B. You're a true genius.

MR. B: Tried and true, Mildred.

MILDRED: All the men I've been with have been geniuses. . . . I'm glad I never went to bed with you, Mr. B. Grateful to have been your raw material.

MR. B: Young. I adore young women. You are no longer young, Mildred. However, your salary will continue until I die. . . . Pas de bouree, my dear, that's the way to exit.

MILDRED: I don't want to exit. I still go to classes every day. I'm ready.

MR. B: I gave you the world. . . . Did you like Monte Carlo? I did Princess Grace's hair there. Ah, the opera house: small, mirrored, baroque and quite enchanting. Jewels sparkled. *Jewels,* our opening night ballet. Remember?

MILDRED: The stage was difficult to work on. Too small. I had to splash Coca-cola on the floor to make it sticky. The stage was so slippery!

MR. B: Yes. I agree; but you dancers enjoyed an intimacy with the audience that only a small house allows. (*Takes a hand mirror out of his attaché case.*) Have a look, Mr. K . . . Bill?

BILL: (*Looks at his haircut.*) I think I like it. It's not done yet, is it?

MR. B: A proper haircut is never done . . . (*Continues haircut.*)

MILDRED: There was a minor tragedy: not enough programs to go around, but I saved one to send to mother.

MR. B: Turn your head, Bill, just a little, that's it.

MILDRED: After the performance there were flowers, lots of flowers.

BILL: It's always been this way, the. . . . Manet's violets . . .

MR. B: What a reception afterwards! At the Hotel de Paris. We all lined up in the lobby to await the Prince and Princess. . . . Once arrived they were delightful . . . untiring throughout the evening, allowing themselves to be questioned and talked to by almost everyone.

MILDRED: Almost everyone.

MR. B: They stayed till the very end. . . . Champagne flowed as well as scotch, gin, vodka . . . and the food was excellent. . . . Memories are made of this.

MILDRED: I presented you with a flower, took it back, and then I gave you the entire bouquet.

MR. B: The progress of a dancer is romantic. Painfully romantic.

BILL: Dancers can be collected like baseball cards or ping-pong balls. Some bounce higher than others, and when they burn they give off noxious odors. In the end they lie twisted, and airless, not even able to roll off the table.

MILDRED: Oh, have you been backstage?

BILL: In my mind, I've been behind the scenes, and seen it all . . . yes.

MILDRED: Once, during rehearsal, I hit my head on a low beam. The gash in my scalp required stitches. Once, during a performance of Apollo two male dancers slipped in the mist. . . . Once, one slipped during the Bizet just as he was catching me. The audience gasped. I've always felt that dancing was dangerous territory.

MR. B: I'm done for now, Mr. K . . . Bill . . . How do you like it?

BILL: (*Looking at himself in mirror.*) I like it. It gives me a sense, as Poe does, of losing my bearings . . . a feeling of an elastic sort of time . . . a heaving floor. As a friend of mine, I call him Rabbit, once remarked, "When a good haircut is over, you don't know what hit you." It's a physical feeling.

MILDRED: When I fought with Mr. X, I knew what hit me.

(*A clear bell sound rings once.* RABBIT *enters. His character is much like Lenny in* Of Mice and Men.)

RABBIT: Tell me what it'll be like, Bill. Will you always stay with me?

(MR. B *brushes hair off* BILL'S *collar. Powders his neck. Removes a cape that he had placed over* BILL *to protect* BILL'S *clothing. He does what barbers do for a customer. He helps* BILL *out of the chair.*)

BILL: (*Introduces* RABBIT.) This is Rabbit. Rabbit, this is the marvelous Mildred, premiere danseuse of the SoHo Ballet Company. And this gentleman is Mr. B, impresario/barber/ choreographer/genius.

MR. B: Rabbit; what an odd name for a human being. Meant affectionately I presume. (*He bows low.*)

MILDRED: I've heard so much about you. The way you quote Edgar Allen Poe. I love you already.

RABBIT: (*To* BILL.) Have they come to put me away? . . . I want to stay with you, Bill.

BILL: They're friends. Don't be afraid of them. . . . Listen, Rabbit, we'll continue as we are: I'll paint and you'll twitch and leap. When you're sad I'll rub your back for you. Whatever I make, I make for you, darling, because I love you. If you could read, you'd find poems dedicated to you in my diary.

RABBIT: Will you stop the Dog star from barking at me?

BILL: I have captured all of astronomy for you, Rabbit. The Dog star whose name is Sirius, is safely behind glass, glued to a thalo blue piece of paper.

MILDRED: (*To* RABBIT.) How do you like Bill's haircut? You haven't said a word about that.

RABBIT: You look good, Bill.

BILL: Thank you, dear . . . Now tell me, what have you been doing while I was getting my haircut?

RABBIT: I loved a parakeet too hard, and then it died.

BILL: Yes, in death the past and the present become one. What has been latent becomes manifest. A force has been tapped and used.

MILDRED: Is that all you have to say, Bill? The man has murdered a bird! Oh-h!

BILL: I have more to say . . . to Rabbit . . . (*Puts his arms around* RABBIT.) A vibration as of a musical pitch came to me from the field where you were playing with the birds. As the sound trembled through the air, a deep rose color seemed to blush and stain the entire atmosphere. Your smile radiates pure bliss, dear Rabbit. It leaves me quite helpless.

MR. B: (*Referring to* RABBIT.) His body leaps about on tiny legs. I can't do a thing with him.

BILL: You may leave the room, Rabbit, and hide my dossier. (*He hands* RABBIT *a dossier.*) One never knows who may want to read what I've written: to read is to misinterpret. Only I have the key.

RABBIT: Yes, Bill.

(RABBIT *exits. The bell note sounds.* MAN *from the CIA enters. He wears a mask or stocking over his face.*)

MAN: You're all under arrest. We've broken the code and know what you're really talking about. You pinkos often disguise yourselves as a deeper shade of rose . . . and it ain't my favorite color. I go for the primaries: red, white, and blue.

BILL: Those are not the primaries. Red, yellow, and blue are.

MAN: I hate yellow!

MILDRED: Who ratted on us? Was it *Ballet Magazine*? Was it Anna Düsseldorf?

MAN: A little birdie told me. A little dead birdie.

MR. B: Dead birds don't sing.

MAN: Ever heard of Albert Einstein?

ALL: No!

MAN: He's the brains behind the brains, right? I pretended to be taken in by his mind control machine, but I'm still here to tell the tale. Don't anybody move. Where's the other agent? Where's third in charge, Comrade Rabbit? I happen to know that this place is not an artist's studio, but a 'drop' for secret information. Your ballet slippers, Miss Mildred Danseuse, have been confiscated and sent to Capezio's for a complete investigation. Why, for instance, did you pin those seemingly innocent little pink ribbons on your toe shoes, instead of having them sewn on?

MILDRED: That's just the way I do it. . . .

MAN: And you, Mr. B! Everyone is well aware that the real Mr. B was Chinese and had ties to Singapore that transcended any loyalty he may have had to American cuisine. Just because you drink champagne from a ballet slipper does not prove that your palate is upper Lincoln Center. You're a spy, Mr. B!

MR. B: Every artist is a spy.

BILL: Look here. Do you have a search warrant?

MAN: (*Pats his jacket pocket.*) Do I ever. . . . So where is this agent, Rabbit? Old pink eyes is what his nickname is, right? Produce old pink eyes right now or I'll break heads, and I don't mean maybe.

MILDRED: Too bad you don't mean maybe. Where there's a maybe there's still some hope.

MAN: (*Twists* BILL'S *arm behind his back.*) You ready to talk?

BILL: It's always been this way, the. . . .

MAN: Think you're too cryptic for me? (*Twists* BILL'S *arm again.*)

BILL: To make a work of art all one needs is an eye and memory.

MAN: If memory is in the mind what do you need an eye for?

BILL: How does memory enter?

MAN: Through a computer?

BILL: I am not a machine.

MAN: All right, Mr. Not-a-Machine, where is the Rabbit?

MR. B: You're making a horrible mistake. Have you tried next door? Does this look like a rabbit hutch to you?

MAN: You've been under surveillance for quite some time. No mistake about the whereabouts of the Rabbit.

(RABBIT *sneaks in. He attacks* MAN. MAN *falls.*)

MILDRED: (*Removes the mask from* MAN'S *face.*) Oh! Oh it's my

X, Mr. X. Is he dead? Tell me you're not dead my hateful one. (*She does some part of the dying swan from* Swan Lake. *We hear* Swan Lake *music.*)

RABBIT: Dance is good. I like dance.

MR. B: You might be able to accomplish some awful version of a jeté, but you will never, ever, ever be able to suspend yourself for a breathless second or two above the stage to do beats, like this! (*He demonstrates beats in the air.*)

MAN: I'm dying, Mildred. Will you come back to me?

MILDRED: Too late, Mr. X. I don't need you. I don't want new furniture. I don't want to pose for your photographs. I don't want to order steak because you can afford it, you nouveau riche fool. You don't understand me, but I understand you. You only want what you can't get. Right now that's me. But you don't love me, not really.

MAN: Too late for anything but a farewell kiss.

MILDRED: Ugh! I shall never kiss a man who is not even a *footnote* to history.

MAN: I love you, Mildred, didn't I buy you a telephone message/recorder?

MILDRED: Bought it, and then took it back when you found out I was receiving messages from your rival for my affections, Mr. G.

MAN: I'm a jealous son of a bitch. Pray for me.

BILL: Nobody prays for an Indiangiver. That's the way it's always been, the. . . .

MAN: Would you please finish that sentence before I die, or I'll come back to haunt you . . . Oh, it's getting darker.

(*Stage lights get slightly darker.*)

MR. B: Before you go to that other place, Mr. X, may I do something clever with your hair? One should look one's best at curtain time. . . . I think you can carry the spiked look, but I'm not sure. Hmmmn?

MAN: What do you charge? I want the most expensive cut you've got.

BILL: Rabbit, get him out of my studio. Take him to the basement . . .

(*To* MR. B.)

Please help Rabbit with Mr. X, Mr. B.

MR. B: (*Helping* RABBIT *to lift* MR. X. *They begin to exit.*) The most expensive cut and styling I do, and this includes a blow-dry, is the Blunt Iago. It insinuates everything and can create quite a stir. You'll be the rage in your coffin. Not a hair out of place.

RABBIT: Man is heavy. Very heavy. Heavy for me to carry. So heavy, Bill.

BILL: Yes, he must be. He has always been, the. . . .

MILDRED: He only looks light, but he carries Mahler in his pocket. The cassette weighs him down . . .

(RABBIT *and* MR. B *carry* MR. X *around the stage, first one leading, then the other going backwards. We hear some heavy Mahler music.*)

MILDRED: If only he had listened to me about Purcell, or Mozart. Just last month he traveled up and down in elevators listening to Muzak, but the man couldn't lighten up . . . . Now he will die to a dirge! (*Hysterical.*) Get him out! Take him away! Remove him from my sight.

RABBIT: Yes. Out. Yes. Out. Yes. Out. Yes. Out.

MR. B: Farewell my lovelies, I've had a simply delightful and engrossing evening.

(*They finally exit. Mahler music stops.*)

BILL: I suppose things don't turn out too happy when they haven't been too good all along.

(*Music from* La Sonnabula (*by Rieti, after Bellini*) *begins.*)

MILDRED: I never believed for a minute that he was from the CIA, they're all up in New England and down in Central America. Why would the CIA come to Utopia Parkway? (*She dances to* La Sonnabula.)

BILL: Ephemera. Living ghost. Sleepwalker. What you have lost I have found. . . . You are my transition piece.

MILDRED: Are you changing your style?

BILL: I'm changing my direction.

MILDRED: I can't speak very well while I am dancing, especially since I am supposed to represent lost youth sleepwalking through life. I can porte de bras, and entrechat, and fall backwards if there is someone to catch me. Gravity is my enemy, Bill . . . and time is no longer on my side.

BILL: *I* am, Mildred. (*He stands behind her.*)

MILDRED: (*Falls backwards into his arms.*) Thank you.

(*Cage-ian music begins (serial-type music, as at opening of play). An amber light antiques the scene.*)

MILDRED: Bill, my dear, do you realize that death in the abstract is life?

(BILL *leads* MILDRED *to a part of the room that then becomes a painting/collage as he arranges things/objects around her. He returns to wooden chair and sits in it in an attitude resembling the way he was sitting at start of play. He observes his 'still life' collage.*)

BILL: One can only extract from the abstract what one puts into it: the Apollinaris kettle spouting steam, Hansa yellow, the leaf, the shell, viridian, magenta, Payne gray, cadmium orange, lace, photographs, the apotheosis, the dedication, the ballerina . . .

(MILDRED *bows deeply. Music stops abruptly.*)

BILL: It's always been this way, the music stops and the play ends.

Blackout

END OF PLAY